How to have a BiBLe MakeoveR

How to have a BIBLE MAKEOVER

Catherine Mackenzie

CF4•K

Dedication:
To my parents William and Carine who
taught me to brush my hair, clean my teeth
and read my Bible. CMM

10 9 8 7 6 5 4 3 2 1

Copyright © 2017 Christian Focus Publications
Paperback ISBN: 978-1-78191-784-8
Epub ISBN 978-1-5271-0054-1
Mobi ISBN 978-1-5271-0055-8

Published in 2017 by
Christian Focus Publications,
Geanies House, Fearn, Tain, Ross-shire, IV20 1TW, U.K.

Cover design by Daniel van Straaten
Illustrations by Jeff Anderson
Printed and bound by Nørhaven, Denmark

Scripture quotations are from The Holy Bible, English Standard Version, copyright © 2001 by Crossway Bibles, a publishing ministry of Good News Publishers. Used by permission. All rights reserved. esv Text Edition: 2011.

Contents

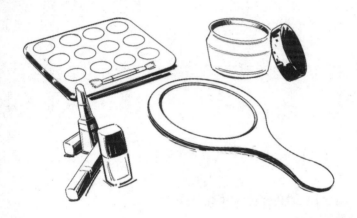

What's a Makeover?

We've all seen these amazing programmes on the television called makeovers. You know the ones – someone is given a hair stylist, a makeup artist and a fashion designer for the day. The guy or girl comes into the studio wearing sweat pants and a T-shirt, then a few hours later they leave looking like a million dollars.

When you think about makeovers do you think ...

    a. Wow! I want one. I can't wait.

    b. Yuck. Hate the idea. That's just torture!

    c. Daahling. Give me the tweezers and tongs

       – I'll give YOU a makeover – you need one!

I think most of you probably said a or b, but if you said c then I'll try and fit you into my diary!

Some people prefer to be let loose with the brushes, others just enjoy the experience. Still others run a mile from anything resembling a lip gloss!

If you were going to be on the receiving end of a makeover what would you expect to happen? If someone has a makeover should they:

    a. Look worse than they did? (What! You've got to be kidding right?)

    b. Look pretty much the same as they did? (Well, what would be the point of that?)

    c. Look totally different, absolutely transformed, and in a mind-boggling, eye-popping way – amazing!

Well, I think if you had been given the undivided attention of three beauty professionals then yes – c is what you should be expecting. The T.V. makeover programmes are all about the change! They want to swap old-fashioned and scruffy for smart and oh so stylish! The guy or gal receiving the makeover should, at the very least, end up being a bit better looking than they were originally. So makeovers are about change and trying to change something for the better.

They sometimes call that a transformation.

Though I wonder ... what would happen if one year down the line the T.V. cameras were to make a surprise return visit to the makeover winner? What would they find? Without a stylist and a designer in their house day in day out, would the makeover last? Would the transformation be a permanent one or not?

Picture this: the cameras and journalists are waiting outside. The door opens. Everyone is anxious to see what the winner of last year's makeover looks like, twelve months on. What would you expect to see?

a. A fashion icon, shiny and spotless and totally on trend.

b. Smart clothes, not too fashionista, but not too shabby either.

c. The sweatpants are back!

a – is perhaps unrealistic.

b – would be nice.

c – well? Yup. It's quite likely, but if it was early on a Saturday morning I might just let them off!

Does Change Last?

You see that's the thing about change or transformation – it doesn't always last. Change can be permanent or it can be temporary. And pretty much any physical transformation is only ever going to be short term. And it's only ever skin deep, as they say.

There is, however, one change or transformation that is permanent – and it's the only one that really matters. It's when God changes you from the inside out. It's a spiritual transformation. There are lots of words that we use for this. You might have heard of some of them:

Conversion   Salvation

Sanctification   Justification

11

Conversion and salvation are two words that are often used when Christians talk about how God changed their lives. Conversion means that you are changed from one thing to another. So, for example, someone might be a fan of one football team and then later on be converted to following another. Perhaps the new team has been winning more games. However, a spiritual conversion is different. It's not just a change of mind on your part; it's God's work. He converts you. He changes you. You're no longer the sinner who focuses on selfishly following your own way. Instead you are someone who believes and trusts in God.

What's Your Status?

Salvation is the result of conversion. Think about salvation as the status of someone who believes that Jesus died to save them from their sin. On social media you are often asked 'What's your status?' So you give a few words that sum up your morning.

Your dad's status might be: I need a coffee!

Your brother might say: Football is the best!

What would your status be?

Well, your spiritual status is either saved or not saved. Think about that. What is your spiritual status? Have you asked God to save you?

The type of change that God is interested in lasts more than a few weeks or months. The Bible wants to give you a makeover for eternity. For ever.

Salvation is a forever change – when a sinner who disobeys God and deserves to be punished is changed to someone who is free from the guilt and punishment of sin ... all because of Jesus!

What has Jesus got to do with it? Well, get out your Bible – you're going to need it.

A Famous Bible Verse

We're going to talk about Jesus quite a bit in this book ... so, to start off, let's look at a famous Bible verse – John 3:16.

For God so loved the world, that he gave his only Son that whoever believes in him should not perish but have eternal life.

This is a quick summary of salvation. It's just twenty-five words and takes you less than a minute to read. But it tells us everything we need to know in a nutshell.

1. Human beings need rescuing. If left to ourselves, we would perish. We are sinners. We are guilty.

Without God's power and forgiveness we are lost.

 **Mini Fact:** What is 'perish'? Well, you'll know this if you've been rooting around at the back of the fridge. Mouldy cucumber, smelly milk ... these have perished. They were meant to be eaten, but now they can't be. There comes a point when a sinner's life has perished. After death there is judgment and unforgiven sinners do not go to heaven; there is no eternal life – it is the opposite. Salvation and forgiveness are only available this side of death and eternity. Destruction and death are the only alternative to God's love and forgiveness. Sinners will perish without God's forgiveness.

2. Remember that although God hates sin, God loves sinners. His love is so great that he gave his only Son (Jesus) to be born into this world, to live a sinless life and then to take the punishment instead of sinners.

3. Those who believe in Jesus Christ, in the power of his death and resurrection, will not be punished for their sin but given everlasting life.

It's About You

You may not have realised this, but John 3:16 is a verse for you. When it refers to the world it's referring to you (and me). All have sinned – every single human being who has ever lived, except for Jesus. So if you are one of those sinners who has not yet trusted in Jesus Christ, or if you are one of those sinners who has – you are one of 'the world'.

If you haven't trusted in Jesus Christ, there is another word that describes you, and that is 'lost'. Someone who goes for a mountain trek without a map and a compass is usually thoroughly lost by the end of the day. Dogs, mountaineers and helicopters will probably be involved! When you are lost you need to be rescued. And someone who is without God's forgiveness is spiritually lost. The rescue plan required is God's rescue plan – Jesus. That rescue plan took place on the cross when Jesus died in the place of sinners. That is the story of salvation, and the story of salvation continues in you, if you turn away from sin and trust in Jesus.

Mirror, Mirror on the Page

So, it's a fact; you need a spiritual transformation – a Bible makeover. Day by day, God wants you to be more like Jesus. And one of the best places to start a Bible makeover is – ta da – in the Bible of course!

Just as every person needs a mirror before they start their make up, you need to read God's Word so you can get the basics sorted. The Bible gives you all the information you need to see what you are really like inside. And that's the important part of you – the part that really matters – your soul. Your soul either loves God or it doesn't. It either believes in God and what he says or it doesn't. And the soul that loves and believes in God is beautiful. Truly and eternally beautiful.

Left on its own, your soul isn't beautiful because it is devoted to itself and its evil desires. You need a spiritual makeover because without that you are lost. But here's a thing – you might get the wrong end of the stick with that word 'lost'. It doesn't mean that God has mislaid you or doesn't know where you are. He knows everything about you! You can't hide anything from the all-knowing God. But when you are spiritually lost, it means that you don't know where you are and that you don't know you need God. When you are lost it's because *you've* messed up – not God.

Now the only one who can help you in this terrible situation is God. There is only one way for your soul to be truly transformed and that is through God's power and God's Word. Reading the Bible, thinking about it, praying to God that he will help you understand it and follow it are important areas in your spiritual life.

But why is a spiritual transformation even necessary? Well, the next chapter will go into that.

Read More: Romans 3:23; Luke 1: 30-33; Romans 8:32-34; Luke 23: 44-47; Luke 24:1-12; Acts 10: 34-43; Isaiah 59:1-2; Ezekiel 18:4; Ephesians 2:4-5.

Think About Jesus: You've just read some verses from Isaiah chapter 59.

These tell us that sin separates us from God. But further on in the chapter we read in verse 20: *A Redeemer will come ... to those who turn from transgression.* This redeemer is the Lord Jesus Christ. To redeem something means that it is bought back. God, who is our creator, has bought or brought back sinners to himself by forgiving their sins. It is through his Son's sacrifice that our sin has been forgiven.

 **Makeover Tip:** The essential thing to realise is that you can't do this makeover yourself. We human beings aren't able to change our spiritual life and we aren't even willing to do it. On our own we love sin and do not love God. But God demands holiness (perfect obedience). He hates sin. We can't obey God by ourselves. Who is to blame for this horrific situation? Well – we are!

Adam and Eve may have been the first people to sin, but we all choose to continue to sin day in, day out. We're responsible for our own problems.

Just because you were born a sinner and can't obey God doesn't give you an excuse to just keep on sinning, doing what you want and not what God wants. God has given you choices. Sinners still have the choice to read God's Word, to listen to the Bible being read, to go to church, but often they choose other things instead of God. You need to cry out to God for help so that he will make you really concerned about your sin. Beg him for help. Sin is a disease and it is deadly. Only God can break its power over you.

Wonderful Women: We're going to focus on a few different Bible women in these sections. But for now the woman or girl I'm going to mention here is you – you are wonderful. Maybe you realise that already. 'I'm great. An all rounder. Nothing phases me.' Fab! But did you know that you are wonderful

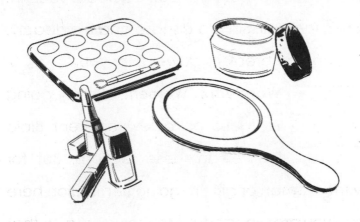

because God made you? And he made you to love him. That should be your function. Your chief aim in life. God made humanity to love and honour him, but sin has spoiled it all. God has the answer though. You must come to him. Talk to God and ask him to help you believe in him, to trust in him and love him. Bring your sin to him and ask him for forgiveness. Because of what Jesus did by dying in the place of sinners, forgiveness is free. Don't forget though, it cost Jesus dearly. He gave his life, he took sin's guilt so that his people could live guilt-free for ever.

Do You Really Need to Wash?

What would you do if you were at a beautician's and someone came in wearing smelly clothes and needing a good scrub yet said to the stylist in charge, 'I don't really need to wash. I took a shower three weeks ago so it's not that necessary.'

a. Would you hold your nose and make your excuses?

b. Would you check your diary? Perhaps something weird has happened and you've inexplicably arrived in the Middle Ages?

c. Would you gently, but firmly, suggest the individual takes your slot and place them in front of the mirror?

Well, everyone in this world is in dire need of a Bible makeover – a permanent inward transformation. Our souls need to be changed. And each and every one of us at some point is so blind we don't see the need for it. We're like that person going

into the beautician's thinking that one shower every three weeks is enough.

Many people think that going to church every now and then is all they need to be a good person and get to heaven. 'I read my Bible.' 'I pray to God – now and then.' 'I don't really need to change. I'm good already. I've not stolen anything. I've never killed. Why do I need to change?'

Do You Get What Sin is?

Well, people who speak like that don't really get what sin actually is. Sin is anything that goes against what God says. And sin is even those times when we don't do exactly what God wants. Sin is big things like murder, thieving and lying. But sometimes we say to ourselves, 'It was only a small lie', 'I only got angry – I didn't hurt anyone.' But the reality is that even our words and thoughts can be sinful. Even one sin is enough to separate us from God.

Mini Fact: God the Father and God the Son are equally involved in salvation. God sent his Son to save sinners – remember? God the Father and God the Son are both merciful and just. Keep in mind that Jesus takes a hard line on sin. He died to save sinners but he doesn't turn a blind eye to our wrongdoing either. He said in the Bible that being angry is the same as murder. Thinking about cheating on your husband or wife is the same as actually doing it.

From Day One

Sin is the situation that every human being is in.
Every person – man, woman and child is a sinner.
The Bible even tells us that unborn children are
sinners. The baby in the womb is, by nature, a
sinner according to Psalm 51:5. That means that
every child is born with the desire to sin. They
may not physically do the wrong things that an
older child or adult can do, but even at the very
beginning of our lives we are born with the desire
to sin in our heart. But God is a God of mercy. He
saves sinners from all nationalities, backgrounds
and ages. God can save anyone. Even someone
who isn't even a day old or a minute old can be
saved by God's power. God can change the
heart of the very oldest and even the heart of
the littlest baby inside its mother.

You don't need to teach a child how to lie! It
just happens. Parents can go to great lengths to
teach a child not to do certain things like being

dishonest, stealing or being selfish. Pretty much everyone recognises that these are not good things to do. But every person starts doing these things by themselves at a very young age. That is because sin is part of us, right from the very beginning.

What's the Standard?

What does the word 'sin' mean? Words are fascinating little things. We're reading this in the English language, but a lot of English words began hundreds of years ago. The word 'sin' is an old English word that means to miss the mark. It was something that was used in the sport of archery when arrows were shot at targets. If the arrow missed, the word 'sin' was called out. Over time this little word came to be used to describe how spiritually we miss the mark when we don't obey God. Every sin we do is something that falls short of what God requires of us. The Bible tells us in the book of Romans: *All have sinned and fall short of the glory of God.*

God's Glory? What does that Mean?

Well, God's glory in this verse means God's perfect standard, his absolute splendid perfection. Another word for that would be his holiness. He is the standard we've all got to match – and we fail miserably. In tennis everyone wants to be the top seed. In athletics everyone wants to be the Olympic medal winner. In football you want to be the captain whose team has won the World Cup. That's because all these people excel at what they do.

Well, God is excellent. He is the most excellent of excellent. And if you aren't like him you can't be with him. And being with the one true perfect loving God is what we should all want. The alternative is simply terrible and horrible.

So when we aren't like God and can't be with him, what's the answer? We can't be like God because, as the Bible says, we've all sinned. And any sin – however small, or big – is against God.

Even the very desire for sin – the fact that you want to do something that God doesn't like – is enough to keep you at arm's length from him. But the situation isn't hopeless. God does have an answer; he wants to change you and he is able to do that. Remember God's rescue plan is Jesus and he completed everything needed for this rescue, when he gave up his life on the cross.

Beautiful or Ugly?

Isn't it true that in the fashion world everyone seems to want a makeover! All the magazine articles are about how you – Miss Ordinary – need to look totally different in order to be Miss Extraordinary. But, in reality, people have different tastes and fashions change. When it comes down to clothes and makeup it's not that necessary to have a makeover. It might be nice, but sometimes even the fashion fans get it wrong and the makeover ends up being a fat fiasco!

But be certain about this, a spiritual trans-formation is absolutely necessary for everyone. We're all sinners. And sin is ugly.

God has given us his law and commands in the Bible and any time we go against that law we're sinning. We are doing evil. Sin is not just something you do; it is something you are. Sin is what you are inside. And it's bad. Only God can deal with it and it's only God who really knows how truly terrible sin is.

I'm sure you've heard about evil. Many people refer to it when they talk about horror movies or ghost stories – particularly at Halloween. It's as though they think evil is just part of a scary story. Something to go 'Oooh' at. Other people talk about evil when they refer to murderers or dictators. It's as though evil is something other people do. 'That guy is an evil monster!' they shout out at the T.V. when a criminal comes on. Although those dark Halloween stories are about evil, and murder and torture are acts of evil, evil is actually any time someone goes against God and his law. If you are defiant and rebellious against God you are being evil.

So let's go back to the beginning and find out how it all went wrong.

The Beginning

God is the creator of the world and when he made it, he saw that it was very good. He was pleased with what he had done. He made an environment that was a perfect place to live. The world had a beautiful unpolluted climate. There was plenty of delicious food to eat and there was no such thing as drought. Adam and Eve were the first man and woman. They were sinless and had a perfect relationship with God.

The whole of creation was like a large statement written across the universe and beyond, saying how good God was, how glorious and wonderful.

Adam and Eve were made in God's image. They were like him in a special, unique way. They were a reflection of God. Hey, we're back to talking about mirrors again! When you stand in front of a mirror you see a reflection of yourself. Adam and Eve were a reflection of God their creator – at least at first.

The image got spoiled. There had been just one commandment they had to follow. God had instructed them not to eat from the tree of the knowledge of good and evil. The garden had been full of trees good for eating. It was just this one tree they were not allowed to eat from. However, the evil one, Satan, in the form of a serpent, persuaded the woman, Eve, to eat from the tree. She persuaded Adam and that was that.

Adam and Eve were no longer in friendship with God. It was as though a great barrier had been raised between them. Adam and Eve were actually scared to be with God – they tried to hide from him. But hiding from the God who can see everything is impossible.

God banished them from the beautiful garden as part of their punishment. Instead of living forever they would one day die. Pain and suffering would be part of their lives and sin would always be there, spoiling everything. Adam and Eve's own sons fell out and one killed the other. From the moment Adam and Eve sinned, every human being born after them would be in rebellion against God.

When they sinned against him, God told Adam and Eve what to expect in the future. It was going to be tough, but one day God would send a Saviour. Yes, he had to punish sin, but he already had a rescue plan in place.

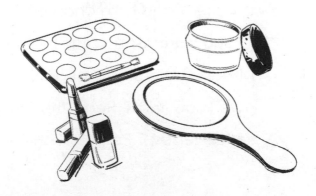

God's plan for a makeover was ready before time even began.

We can call this makeover salvation. And the foundation of it is Jesus!

More about that in the next chapter!

 **Wonderful Women:** What about Eve? Yes, she was the first human to sin, but she was also the first human God spoke to about salvation, when he told Eve that one of her descendants would crush the serpent. The serpent was the evil one, the devil. Someone would, in the future, come from Eve's family tree to defeat him. That someone is Jesus Christ, God's Son. We can read Jesus' family tree in Matthew chapter 1 and Luke chapter 3.

 **Read More:** God's plan for salvation began before time began. How do we know that? Read the following Bible verses: 1 Peter 1:13-21

 **Think About Jesus:** God is one God in three persons. The three persons are God the Father, God the Son and God the Holy Spirit. They are all involved in creation because in the story of creation we read that God says, 'Let us make man in our image.' It is not 'Make man in my image.' Jesus is our Creator as well as our Saviour.

Makeover Tip: Do you realise that you need a spiritual makeover? You need to change in order to please God. So although God does this work in you, what you need to do is:

1. Read the Bible – it is God's Word to you.

2. Pray that God will help you understand it.

3. Ask God for the faith you will need to believe his Word and obey it.

a FoReVeR HoMe

If you were given the opportunity to save the life of a stray dog at risk from a dangerous situation, what would you do? What do you think would be the best way to go about things?

a. Get it out of the dangerous spot and then let it go.

b. Get it out of the dangerous spot and then take it to a dog rescue centre.

c. Get it out of the dangerous spot, take it to a dog rescue centre and then give it a forever home.

I think we would all like to give the stray dog a forever home. That would be a truly happy ending.

I love stories about rescues. I saw a video clip of four guys lifting a dog to safety from a river, but the dog didn't stop to say thank you at the end. He just legged it. Some dogs are rescued by animal centres. The poor creatures come in looking very sick, but after a bit of tender loving care, a few weeks later they look totally different. Bright eyed and bushy tailed! However, it's not always easy to find homes for them. One story I heard recently was about how a dog was rescued and given a good home, but a few months later he had to return to the dog centre as his owner was moving abroad. Thankfully, the dog was given a second chance by another owner. The dog was rescued twice.

God wants to rescue sinners like you and me. That's what we call salvation: God's rescue plan. But God's rescue plan is faultless – it's not going to need a re-run. When you are saved, you are saved!

Back to Basics

Do you remember the verse we read before, John 3:16? The gospel in twenty-five words: *For God so loved the world, that he gave his only Son, that whoever believes in him should not perish but have everlasting life.*

Let's go through that once again. The basics of God's rescue plan called salvation are:

1. Our need – we're sinners. Our sin separates us from God. We need to be forgiven.
2. God's love – God wants to rescue us from our sin and he can. He is willing and able to forgive us.
3. God's action – he sent Jesus, his only Son.
4. Jesus' action – he obeyed God, his Father, and lived a perfect life without sin instead of

us. He also died on the cross, taking God's punishment on himself instead of us.

5. The result – those who believe in Jesus won't perish but have everlasting life.

We all deserve punishment from God because we are sinners. But God has given a way of escape from punishment. How did he do that? He made a rescue plan before the beginning of the world. His Son would take all the punishment. He would take the guilt. But, in order to do this, he had to come to this earth and be born as a human being – a wriggling, crying, squirming, dribbling baby. Don't believe the Christmas carols when they say, 'No crying he makes.' Jesus was a human baby and babies have to cry. They wouldn't be human otherwise. Babies need to cry in order to stretch their lungs and get them working. If babies didn't cry, people would forget about them. Crying is very important for babies. So when Jesus was a baby he made as much noise as any other little boy or girl. Jesus was – and is – completely human and completely God.

Jesus had to live the perfect life that we couldn't live, but living a perfect life was not enough. He had to take the punishment for sin as well. The punishment that should have been ours was placed on him.

You could call this – The Ultimate Makeover! The guilt for sin was given to Jesus and so he was punished. The righteousness of Jesus was given to sinners and so they were freed. God looks at those sinners who trust in Christ and he says 'You are righteous'. This is a very important part of salvation. It's called justification. It's just as if we had never sinned. All those who are brought to believe in Jesus Christ are washed clean from the guilt of sin.

Court Room Drama

Imagine you are in a court room. Someone has been accused. They are the criminal. A judge

is standing at the front ready to pronounce a sentence. But then there is another person there – let's call this person an advocate (or a lawyer). He is standing up for the accused. The advocate says to the judge, 'Let me take the prison sentence instead.' And the criminal goes free.

This doesn't really happen in court rooms today. But it does happen in God's court room.

We're the criminals. God is the judge. Jesus is the advocate. Because of God's plan and Jesus' sacrifice, those who trust in Jesus are no longer unforgiven criminals in God's eyes. Jesus says, 'Let me take their punishment instead.' Sinners don't have to suffer the penalty that they deserve. They just have to trust that Jesus' sacrifice is all that is needed to free them from the guilt and punishment of sin. That is all that is required. God even gives sinners the faith to be able to do that! It's gift after gift after gift with God!

But pay attention! Salvation is more than just a get out of jail free card. It's more than just escaping hell. Yes, heaven is a reward and hell is punishment, but salvation is more than not going to hell. When you are saved, the penalty of hell is taken away but so is the pollution of sin.

Pollution Stinks!

We hear a lot about pollution today. It seems to be everywhere and causing a lot of problems.

We see oil pollution on the news and seabirds and animals suffer a lot from that. We read articles about pollution, describing rubbish littering the countryside. Air pollution not only makes our environment smell bad, it can bring problems to health by giving people breathing difficulties.

There is also a spiritual pollution. Sin pollutes our lives. It gives us a bitter spirit. It makes us selfish, angry, greedy. It gets into every area of our life: our friendships, families, pleasures, work ... Everything, in one way or another is spoiled in some way, by sin. But salvation delivers us from the pollution of sin and it rescues us from the power of sin.

You will notice when you trust in Jesus that you will hate sin more and love God more. That's part of the transformation. That's part of the Bible makeover. You might have struggles. You might actually think, 'I'm sinning more now than I ever was.' But that is often because when God begins a spiritual makeover, he makes you more aware of sin than you ever were before. God wants you to be transformed to become more and more like Jesus. Day by day, by day. Little by little, by little you'll grow, grow, grow to be more like God's Son.

Now, don't think that this transformation is just something that is going to happen to you without any effort on your part. God does change you, but he also gives you the power to work at changing yourself. Keep that in mind as we go on through this Bible makeover journey. This transformation we're talking about is not an excuse to sit back and say, 'God will do everything. I can just lay back and be lazy.' No, that's not what's going to happen.

This transformation will involve you. It's a process. You know what I mean ... Just like a baby who is learning to crawl, then walk, then one day run – a Christian, someone who believes in Jesus, learns to be more like him.

There is a point when you are a sinner and aren't saved – and then God does his special work – and you are saved. That part of salvation can only be done by God but salvation doesn't just stop there and then. Salvation and something called sanctification are joined together. Sanctification is the continuing work of salvation in your life. Yes, when God saves you, you're saved, but God continues his work in you until it is completed.

Salvation and sanctification, you don't get one without the other. You can't separate them.

Heaven? What is it?

We mentioned heaven before. So what is it? Well, it's a place. It's a beautiful place. And it's a place without sin. So how can sinners fit in to a place like that?

Well, remember for a makeover to truly work the makeup has to be put on each day and the clothes pressed and the shoes shone. A true makeover doesn't just happen once – it has to happen every day.

A Bible makeover is the same. Yes, salvation is something that happens once. It's a work that God does, but it's also a work that he keeps doing. God keeps working in us. He keeps making this new and wonderful salvation part of our daily lives. If you trust in Jesus and believe that he has saved you from sin, God is making you more like Jesus – he is making you Christ-like. Bit by bit, day by day.

It's all part of God's plan for taking us to our forever home. HEAVEN.

Not everybody goes there. There isn't an open ticket you can buy because of what you've done or not done in this life. Even the smallest sinful thought or action is enough to keep us out of God's friendship. Sin separates us from God and so it keeps us out of heaven. God's forgiveness redeems us, takes us back and into his family, giving us heaven and eternal life. That's the truth.

The Bible tells us that heaven is so perfect we can't even imagine how great it is.

But what about Hell?

Think of all the good things we have in this world – well they won't be there in hell. The Bible tells us that there is only weeping and anger there. And nobody from hell can ever go to heaven. There is a huge divide between the two places that just can't be crossed.

Thankfully, for as long as you live on this earth you have an opportunity to cross from sin to salvation because of what Jesus did on the cross. Ask God to give you the faith to believe in him and his Word. Ask God to show you how much you need his forgiveness and ask him to take you and transform you day by day to be more like Jesus.

Wonderful Women: One woman who believed in Jesus doesn't have a name in the Bible; she is only known as 'a sinful woman'. She knew how sinful she was and was very upset about it. She wanted to thank Jesus for his love. God had shown her how much she needed forgiveness for her sins and how it was through Jesus, God's Son, that she could be

forgiven. The sinful woman wept so much that her tears washed Jesus' feet. She dried his feet with her hair. The woman didn't mind who saw her. She just wanted to give glory to God.

Sometimes we think that we have to be good before we can be saved, but the Bible tells us that Jesus came to save the ungodly. Not even our good works are good enough to save us. What we have to do is trust in Jesus and his sacrifice on the cross. That is what will save us ... God's work, not ours. The sinful woman believed that. She saw how wicked her sin was and she wept over it. She came to Jesus and worshipped him. Her act of worship was a sign that God had saved her.

 **Makeover tip:** When God shows you that you are a sinner, he gives you a longing to be saved, to be made friends with God. When this happens, come to God to thank him for Jesus' sacrifice and ask God for forgiveness. God will give you good

works to do that will please him. When you are saved you will want to please God. A sign that a baby is growing is when he begins to crawl and then walk and then run. A sign that a Christian is growing is when they love to please God more and more.

Read More: Luke 7: 36-50.

Think about Jesus: Have you ever seen a gardener at work? Sometimes he prunes the tree by taking away unnecessary or dead leaves and branches. Sometimes he does something different – he grafts in new branches. This is when new branches are joined to the trunk of the tree. They eventually become part of the tree, grow into the body of the tree and produce fruit. The Bible describes Jesus like a tree and those who believe in him like the branches of that tree.

Just as the branches that are added to the tree become the tree, so those who believe in Jesus will become like Jesus. The branches of the tree get their strength from the tree. We will get our strength to become holy from God.

a Bigger Problem than Pastries

So the beauty team are back at the beginning again. They've returned to find their winner is still wearing the scruffy tracksuit. To make matters worse, the winner can't be bothered with a healthy diet. The rubbish bin is full of the evidence: fizzy pop cans and microwave meal cartons. What's a health-guru-dietician-beauty-magnet to do? Well, what would you do?

How to have a Bible Makeover

1. Start again from the beginning? (Sigh! All that time wasted.)

2. Give them a different look. (Perhaps they just didn't like the last style?)

3. Give them the skills they need to keep the makeover going. (Face cloth, bar of soap, toothbrush – check!)

Number 3 might be the right way to go if the problem is that they just don't know the facts. However, perhaps it is something more than that. This person possibly needs a full-time body-beauty-guard, so that every time they even look at a pastry they get told what's what. (If such a person exists, I think I need to employ one!)

But when we're talking about a spiritual makeover, it's a far more serious problem than just pastries!

Remember how we talked about what sin is and that sin is not just about actions, it's about thoughts and desires. Sin is actually our identity.

We're born sinners. We are sinners. So, in actual fact, we can try as hard as we can not to sin, but because we are sinners we will sin. Sin, sin, sin, sin, sin! YUCK.

Someone who needs a body makeover can eventually learn the tricks of the trade, like good colour choices and a nice hair-do. But people in need of a spiritual makeover can't do it on their own, they can't actually do it at all. They need God!

The Bible tells us that a leopard can't change its spots. What that means is that a sinner can't change his or her nature. A spiritual makeover – or salvation – is God's work. He saves us.

Everything We Need

But remember that salvation is accompanied by sanctification and God wants us to get involved in that. Yes, he is the only one who can save us. He's the one who changes you from sinner to saved. But God wants those he saves to work at becoming more like Jesus. So, how can weak sinners like us do that? Again, God is the answer. He gives you the power – his power. In fact, to become a Christian and to grow as a Christian God gives you everything you need.

1. Faith
2. Forgiveness
3. Fortitude – I've just made that an F because I think it's clever; it really means power, or strength.
4. Freedom

God gives us faith. So when we believe in God we must thank God. He has given us the faith or ability to believe. God forgives us. Another reason to praise him.

God provides us with fortitude – power and strength to continue at this work of growing as a Christian. God is so good!

Freedom! Right – shout that out like you're a warrior who has just won a battle. You can beat your chest a little if you want. War paint is optional! But thanking God isn't!

Sanctification Means?

We learned earlier about the word Justification – that is when God takes away the penalty of sin so that we're no longer guilty. It's the point when God says, 'You can have eternal life. It's yours.'

Sanctification is when God takes away the pollution and the power of sin. The word sanctification in the Bible has several meanings such as:

Set apart: God has a special purpose for those who believe in him. He has special work for them to do. He sets them apart for this work. Say, for example, someone has been trained as a medic and is skilled at climbing – they might be set apart for a special job in mountain rescue. Someone would see how good they were at medicine and climbing and they'd say, 'This is the job for you. Don't spend your time stacking shelves in the supermarket.'

God sets his people apart. When they believe in him, he wants them to fulfil their purpose. He sets them apart to grow more like Jesus. They are given the special and particular job of giving glory to God.

Cleansed and Purified: This means that God takes away the desire to be sinful. He washes away the love of sin. God replaces the desire to sin with a longing to please God. He takes away the guilt of sin and replaces it with the righteousness of Christ.

Adorned: Adorned is a special word. It means to be made beautiful. It is often used to describe a bride on her wedding day. A woman will spend a lot of time on her clothes and jewellery when she is getting married. She wants to look beautiful for the bridegroom – whom she loves.

There is a lovely verse in a hymn which says:

'The bride eyes not her garments
but her dear bridegroom's face.

I will not gaze at glory

but on my King of grace.'

What this verse means is that as a Christian our greatest love is Christ. Christians, those who believe in Christ, want to be spiritually beautiful for God. They want to be a delight to him. They want to give him glory – tell everyone how wonderful he is. They want to be useful to God too, to give their lives to him. They want to give glory to God. And the best way to glorify God is by obeying him.

God changes us when he saves us. We are no longer lost sinners. We're saved believers. He gives us the strength to love him more, to serve him more and to enjoy him more forever.

Whose Work?

Some people think that it's the good things they do that will save them. But that's wrong.

We're not saved by good works – we're saved for good works. When God forgives you and you become part of his family he has special works for you to do. Remember we were talking about being set apart by God for special work. As a believer your heart will long to please him, not because by doing this you will be saved. No. Your heart will long to please God because he has saved you already.

When God continues to work in our lives, changing us to be more like Christ, he does several things.

God Sustains Us: God gives us the strength we need to please and obey him, to do that special work he has for us to do. What kind of special tasks does God have for us? Well, these can be lots of things. Maybe you think working for God means leaving your home and going as a missionary to a far country. That can certainly be the case. God has sent many people to foreign countries to work as doctors or to translate the Bible into other languages. He also sends some people just down the road to work in a factory, in a family, or in their local church.

One missionary, Helen Roseveare, went to the Congo in Africa to work as a medical doctor. After she had suffered much at the hands of cruel men she could still say that all that suffering had been worth it because Jesus was worthy. God sustained her through her troubles.

When I knew Helen first, it was after she had returned to the United Kingdom. She was working in Northern Ireland with her local church and youth groups. God had sent her abroad as a missionary at first and then he had sent her to her home country. God can send you far away to work for him and he can give you work closer to home.

God Develops Us: Developing is an important part of growing up. When you start to learn a musical instrument, it usually doesn't sound that good, but with practice and teaching you get better. Then one day people actually want to listen to you play and might even applaud loudly at the end. That's what it means to develop. You can develop as a Christian too, by reading God's Word, listening to godly preaching, spending time in prayer and with other Christians. As you develop as a Christian you should find that you are able to teach others about God.

God Perfects Us: And then God perfects us – the work he began is going to be completed one day. There will be a day when every one of God's people will be without sin. It won't happen when we are alive on this earth. Perfection and being without sin is what a Christian has to look forward to after death – when they finally get to heaven.

New Born Baby

Just now, particularly if you are a new believer, you're like a spiritual baby. A baby has all its parts when it is born, but they are just not fully developed. The legs, arms, hands and eyes aren't fully mature. Not yet. The other week I was watching a friend's little baby girl rolling around on the carpet. She knows that she wants to crawl. She wants to get over to that toy on the other side of the room. She's pushing her arms and legs, but she can't quite coordinate everything. So close but not quite ready. Next week will probably be different and I'll get a text saying, 'She's done it! She's on the move!'

So it is with a new Christian. While we are still in this world we know some things about God but not all things. We know how to please God in some ways but not perfectly. We are saved. God will give us eternal life. But God still has to help us to grow to be like Jesus. We know in our heads what God wants, but sometimes we just don't manage to do it. But one day all the dots will join together. We'll know that we need to please God. We'll know how to please God and because we are without sin we will please God – forever! Heaven will be our home and we will be ready for it.

Renovation

Have you ever seen a renovation show on T.V.? It's a makeover show for houses. People find a building that's falling down. Wires are sticking out everywhere. The walls are crumbling. Then they set to work. Because it's a T.V. programme, it seems like just moments later the house is transformed. Everything is perfect. In fact, it's not just structurally sound, it actually looks gorgeous!

That's what God does to our souls. He does a renovation or a remodel. He makes us inwardly holy. We then love God and we're willing to obey him. Before that we only loved ourselves and wanted to do our own thing. After God's salvation, instead of thinking, 'I'm number one!', we know that God is the most important.

Have you ever made a jelly mould? My mum used to have one in the shape of a bunny rabbit. When you shook it out, the jelly took on the shape of the rabbit. It was pretty cool. When God transforms us, he moulds our hearts into a different shape – a God shape. Our hearts become more willing to do what he wants us to do.

The Bible tells us that you will know if someone is really a Christian by the fruit in their lives. What sort of fruit is that? Well, a good tree grows good fruit, while a rotten tree grows rotten fruit. The Bible tells us that God's good fruit – the fruit of the Spirit is: love, joy, peace, patience, kindness, goodness, faithfulness, gentleness and self-control. These are the things that shout out: 'Spiritual makeover accomplished!'

 **Read More:** Galatians 5:22-26; Romans 6:19

 **Wonderful Women:** Dorcas was a wonderful woman, well-loved by the other Christians in her town. She was an example of kindness and goodness. She did a lot for others. This shows us that a spiritual

transformation involves actions as well as words. It's important to tell others about Jesus, but we should also show Jesus by our actions. Don't just talk about love – do loving deeds. Dorcas helped others by using her talent with a needle and thread. She made clothes for people who would have found it very difficult to buy new clothes when they needed them. We should ask God to help us to be inwardly holy, so that our lives will be outwardly holy. Ask God to show you how to be a living day to day example of Jesus.

 **Makeover Tip:** Salvation and sanctification – this is all a wonderful inward transformation. It's a spiritual makeover, but it actually affects the outside too. Our soul influences what our body does. The body and the spirit can be changed by God's Bible makeover. You will find that the closer you come to God, the more you want to do his will, the less you will want your body to sin. You will still struggle with sin, but remember if you didn't have God in your life you probably wouldn't care either way. Struggling with sin can be a sign that God is at work inside you, making you hate sin rather than love it as you once did.

God is wanting to make you holy because he is holy. He wants to make you holy inside, which is when you hate sin and love his ways. He wants you to be holy on the outside, which is when you run away from sin and run towards good actions, thoughts and words.

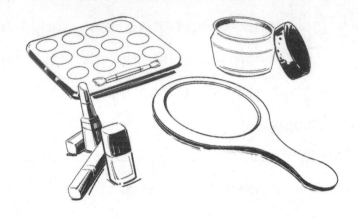

Think About Jesus: The best example of obeying God is Jesus himself. If you want to find out how to please God think about who pleased him the most. It was his one and only Son, Jesus Christ. It is the life of Jesus that will show us how to obey and please God. God the Father has now exalted his Son above all others. After Jesus took the punishment for sin, God raised him to life and then raised him to heaven where he is now. He is in heaven at God the Father's right hand.

it's Not a ONe OFF

You might think this is a strange question or you might think it's a very sensible question: 'Why would someone want a makeover in the first place?'

a. Perhaps they're going out to buy some milk and just can't go out in public unless they look perfect? (Hmm ... what kind of shops are they going to?)

b. They need to visit their granny. (Well, I'm sure their granny would be very pleased to see them no matter how they looked.)

c. They've been invited to a wedding. In fact it's a royal wedding and they're the guest of honour. (O.K. then! If they're going to meet the queen I understand the need for a makeover!)

But remember God's makeover is different. If you're getting ready to meet the queen it's probably just going to be a one off event. So the makeover is simply to get you ready for that big event. God's makeover is not a one off! God's salvation lasts for ever. He wants you to give your life to him. So all this means that salvation and being a Christian is not just for a day. It's not just bits and pieces of your life here and there. It's a forever commitment.

The Thief

And here's a thing to think about ... God can save you and take you to heaven immediately, he can save you and sanctify you over a longer period of time. As Jesus was crucified, two other men were crucified on either side of him. Both were criminals. One was bitter and shouted at Jesus, while the other realised that he was a sinner and asked Jesus to forgive him. Jesus forgave that man: 'Today you will be with me in Paradise.' Moments before, that thief had been an unforgiven sinner, but he was saved and ready for heaven as soon as Jesus had forgiven him. It wasn't a long process. The thief on the cross was saved and went to heaven that very same day.

God saves many people from many backgrounds and though salvation is the same for everyone, it can happen in different ways. Paul was saved very dramatically on the road to Damascus. There was a flash of lightning. He heard the voice of Jesus and he believed. He didn't go to heaven that day like the thief did. God had other work for Paul to do.

Then there is the story of Lydia. It wasn't a sudden or dramatic incident for her. Lydia's heart was opened by the Lord. These words make me think of a flower gently opening in the sunlight. She came to know things about God over time and then she heard the truth about Jesus and trusted in him.

So if you're worried about how long it is going to take God to get you ready for heaven – don't be. If you have trusted in God, you are saved through God's work and Christ's sacrifice. Nothing else needs to be done to get you to heaven. Salvation and sanctification don't need a long time. They just need God's amazing power.

God has Finished it!

When Jesus died on the cross, he said three important words, 'It is finished.' Remember those words if you start thinking I've got to do this or that to get to heaven. Jesus has done it all.

But God is also doing it all. Salvation has been done and is being done. God wants to change you for your own good. He wants to change you so that you can enjoy him more and more. He has saved you and is changing you so that you can give glory to God.

Keep reading God's Word so that God can put his Word into your heart and mind. When God's Word is there, he can prompt you when you need to make the right choice. God is equipping you with faith, strength and his Word, so that you will grow as a Christian and become more like Jesus. God is making sure you are involved in this Christian life – so that you're not just a lifeless puppet. You are a real, living Christian making real choices and decisions. Giving real glory to God.

Why does he do it this way? I'm not exactly sure. I think it's a bit like a parent who allows a 'toddler' to help. Maybe it would be quicker for the parent to do all the work, but they let the child help because it is good for them and helps them learn. God involves us because it is good for us. But most importantly it gives him glory. When we make an effort to please God it shows anyone who sees it that God is worthy.

The War is Won

So what's next? Well, you've read the word 'struggle' a couple of times in this book already. Sin and trying not to sin can be hard. It's a struggle. Sin is still there in your heart and life, even when you have trusted in Christ. Even though God has won the war over sin and he has the victory, there are still skirmishes and battles going on in your life.

However, if you trust in Christ that means you are alive in God and so there is someone else inside you – his name is God the Holy Spirit.

When Jesus rose from the dead, he said something truly wonderful to his disciples. He told them that when he left to go back to heaven, he would not leave them without any comfort. He would send the Holy Spirit to them.

When you trust in Jesus, the Holy Spirit enters your heart and he begins a new work in you.

Remember how we talked about when you trust in Jesus you will find, over time, that things change. You will love God more. You will love sin less. You will love God's Word, praying and spending time with other people who love God.

You will even find that your mind changes. You will find you spend more time thinking about God. Perhaps in the past you disagreed with what it said in the Bible, but when God starts a work in you, you will find that your mind agrees with God.

With all these wonderful things God is doing, what a lot we owe him. Isn't he wonderful? Why wouldn't we want to give our life to him and serve him? Satan doesn't deserve anything from us.

If you haven't trusted in God because you think you'd be missing out, then how wrong you are.

Someone once told me about a girl who had two different boyfriends. The first one was a real meanie. He was always lying to her and causing her trouble. He would take her money and never give it back. He would take advantage of her and never give her anything in return. She eventually told him she wasn't interested. She didn't want to see him anymore.

Good decision.

Eventually she met another young man who was entirely different. He actually loved her. They spent time together and had fun. He was good to her and looked out for her. He didn't treat her badly. In fact her life was great because she'd met him. They decided to get engaged to be married.

Good decision.

The girl is happy because of that young man, whereas before she was unhappy because of the other man.

We need to realise that sin is the real root of unhappiness in our life and that God is the real source of joy. We need to turn away from sin and turn towards God. Good decision!

Sin is Real

We owe our eternal happiness to God. So why would we ever want to continue to muck around with sin? We owe it nothing! It's wrong to think that sin is going to give you any real joy. It's a wretched poison and you don't want it in your life. Imagine someone has given you a glass of water and said, 'There's a tiny bit of poison in this – but just a little.' You wouldn't say, 'Oh well, it's just a little. I'll drink it.' So why deliberately choose to play around with sin in your life. Get away as quick as you can!

It is a sad reality that sin still exists. It's there, lurking in the back of our lives, sometimes making its way right to the front. Perhaps you know that you've been saved by God, you do trust in Jesus yet there are days when you feel, 'I haven't really changed at all. I might even be getting worse! God is so pure and I know that I am not.'

Well, when an unbeliever sins, they either aren't bothered about it at all or they are only concerned about the punishment.

When a believer sins, they are concerned about how that sin is polluting their life and separates them from God. They are concerned that they are not pleasing God.

The closer we are to God, the more we see our sin. It's like a light is being shone on our lives. We see sin for what it really is – ugly and wrong. When God changes us, he opens our spiritual eyes. We realise how shameful our sin is. So, when someone is very troubled about their sin, it is often because they are seeing it better than they did before. Perhaps someone who is the most concerned about their sin, is actually someone who is loving and obeying God.

Upset about Sin?

The Bible tells us about a man named Job. He had a lot of troubles and God allowed many horrible things to happen to him – even though God declared him to be a sincere and upright man. Job, however, said something quite different, 'I am vile' (Job 1:8; 40:4).

Daniel was also greatly beloved by God. In Daniel chapter 10 verse 19 we read that Daniel said that he was 'corrupted'.

So here are two men who we know loved God and were loved by him, yet they are upset about their sin.

This tells us that when someone trusts in God the battle with sin is not over. The Christian's greatest heartache can be when they realise they still have so much sin in them. But one day those who trust in Christ will be without sin. It's just that sometimes Christians see their dirty hearts very clearly and it can be upsetting. We should be thankful though that God shows us our sin, because that means we see how important God's salvation is.

It's Laundry Day!

Some people still peg out their laundry on the line to dry. So imagine you have a large pile of white sheets that have just been cleaned. It's a dry, sunny day so you attach them to the clothes line and wait until the sun dries them while you go inside. However, because it's winter, a sudden fall of snow comes down. You go outside and the sheets that appeared so white an hour ago now actually look grey and drab. The bright whiteness of the snow shows the sheets as not being that white after all.

That's what happens for a Christian sometimes. When they see God and his purity, they realise that their hearts need to be made cleaner.

Open the Window

When you are an unbeliever, your life is like a dark room. The lights are out. The curtains are shut. How do you get rid of the darkness?

Do you try and take some whitewash and make the room white inside? Would it be bright then? (No, still dark).

Perhaps you should try and chase the darkness out. Catch it and sweep it into the bin. (Now that's getting ridiculous.)

Did you think about opening the window? (Yes – the window – let the light in. Simple really when you think about it. But I'm sure you had that answer already.)

But that's the way you deal with the darkness of your spiritual life. This is how you deal with sin – you let the light in. You let Jesus in. He is the only one who can deal with your sin!

Wonderful Women: One wonderful woman in the Bible is called Martha, but her story doesn't start off that great. She and her brother and sister were friends of Jesus and showed him hospitality. But Martha put more importance on the cooking and serving than on listening to what Jesus had to say. Her sister Mary, on the other hand, wanted to make sure she didn't miss a word Jesus said. She stayed close to Jesus to hear him speak. Martha got annoyed and ordered Jesus to tell her sister to help her in the kitchen. Jesus told Martha that it was more important to learn about God than to get all the dishes done. Later on we see a different Martha.

When her brother died she said to Jesus that she knew that one day Lazarus would rise from the dead. She had obviously been listening to what Jesus said and believed in the resurrection. This shows us that when we listen to God's Word we are changed for the better. God's Word is the key to a Bible makeover. Martha began life with the wrong focus, but listening to Jesus and paying attention to his Word changed her.

 **Makeover Tip:** The Word of God is an important piece of equipment for a Bible makeover. Colossians 3:16 tells us that we are to *'Let the Word of Christ dwell in you richly, teaching and admonishing one another in all wisdom.'* This means that there are positive and negative things involved in a Bible makeover just as there are in a physical makeover. A hairdresser might style your hair, but they also might have to untangle it first. When

you are having a spiritual makeover, God has to convict you of your sin and then encourage you to trust and follow him.

Read More: 2 Timothy 3:14-17

Think about Jesus: Jesus is unique because he is God and man. It is because he is God and without sin and a human being that he could take the punishment for sin. Nobody else could. The only way God's anger against sin could be satisfied was when Jesus was punished instead of sinners. Jesus was able to take the punishment and he was willing. God the Father gave his only Son and the Son gave his life. We must give them thanks and glory.

aRe YoU ReaLLY a WaRRioR?

What kind of things do you think a makeover artist really needs?

a. Mirror, makeup, magazines?

b. Fashions, face packs, free food?

c. A sword, a shield and ... what?

Well, a and b are maybe the crucial items for one of those temporary makeovers everyone's going on about ... (if there was free food I would go!) but swords and shields? Well, you don't see those things in a hairdressers, but a Bible makeover is different. Remember how God saves us, but he also equips us, that though salvation is God's work he involves us. A Bible makeover is more defensive than decorative. We're not just puppets on strings; we're actually soldiers. We're fighting against sin and, to do this, God gives us the right tools for the job.

Chuck out the nail files girls, a Bible makeover needs a serious weapon. The Christian life is a battle and we need to put on God's armour to survive the devil's attacks. Here is the kit you need to fight sin.

The Belt of Truth

'Take up the whole armour of God ... fasten on the belt of truth' (Ephesians 6: 13-14).

We need to read God's Word and learn from it. We need to take every opportunity to get strength from the Word of God. Just as a belt kept all of

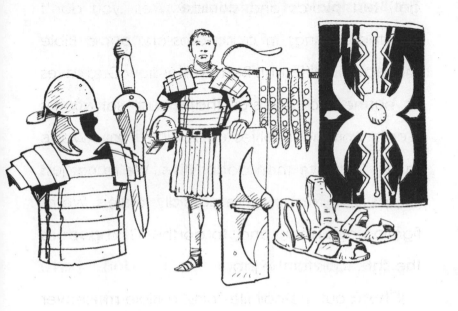

a soldier's clothes and armour in place, so the belt of truth – God's Word – keeps our Christian life in place. If we neglect God's Word, things start falling apart. We make wrong decisions, get confused and we'll start to believe in lies. Some people say if we don't believe the truth we'll believe in anything. God's Word is truth. Read it! It's the only way you will know what to believe and what not to believe.

The Breastplate of Righteousness

'... and having put on the breastplate of righteousness' (Ephesians 6: 14).

A breastplate protects the heart of the warrior. The heart is vital as it pumps blood around the body. If it is injured then the rest of the body gets sick quickly. The heart is essential for life.

The breastplate of righteousness is important for the Christian warrior. Sinners don't have righteousness. Without it no one can have eternal life. But God looks on those whom his Son has saved and, instead of seeing their sin, he sees his Son's righteousness.

Turn from sin to the one true God and to Christ your loving Saviour. For eternal life, you must put on the breastplate of Christ's righteousness.

Shoes of the Gospel of Peace

'... and, as shoes for your feet, having put on the readiness given by the gospel of peace' (Ephesians 6:15).

An army marches on its feet. So an important part of a soldier's kit are boots. Paul describes a part of the Christian's armour as being 'shoes of the gospel of peace'.

The gospel is another word for good news – and the good news that Paul tells us about is the good news of Jesus Christ.

We read about this good news in the Gospel of John, *'For God so loved the world that he gave his only Son, that whoever believes in him should not perish but have eternal life'* (John 3:16).

But here's another verse that is full of good news: *'For I am sure that neither death nor life, nor angels nor rulers, nor things present nor things to come, nor powers, nor height nor depth, nor anything else in all creation, will be able to separate us from the love of God in Christ Jesus our Lord'* (Romans 8:38-39).

And another! *'For while we were still weak, at the right time Christ died for the ungodly ... but*

God shows his love for us in that while we were still sinners, Christ died for us' (Romans 5:6, 8).

Without the gospel there is no hope or peace. But the gospel of Jesus Christ gives a certain hope of heaven and a peace in your hearts. You can trust God. He is in control. Another way of saying this is – he is sovereign – he rules.

Are you one of those girls with twenty sets of pumps and plimsolls exploding out of your closet? If so, you probably think that shoes are vital, but even then you might not think that shoes are life-savers. However, if you walk for any distance with shoes that don't fit, then you'll soon know how painful it can be. You'll have blisters before very long. A soldier on the battlefield, who has to march for miles, needs well-fitting shoes – strong ones. Without them he will be in danger from the enemy. His shoes could be a matter of life or death.

Without the message of the gospel of Christ, a Christian has nothing. Without the good news of Jesus Christ, Christians would have no peace and no hope. Without the gospel all would be lost.

The Shield of Faith

'In all circumstances take up the shield of faith, with which you can extinguish all the flaming darts of the evil one' (Ephesians 6:16).

Mostly armour is about defence. In the old days a shield would stop arrows from piercing the warrior. The Christian's shield is called the shield of faith. God gives us the gift of faith because with it you will 'extinguish all the flaming darts of the evil one'.

The evil one is the devil, but what are the flaming darts?

In battles long ago there would be archers who would shoot arrows or darts into the opposing army. Sometimes they would set the arrows on fire in order to cause further injury or damage. But if soldiers used their shields they would be able to fend off those fiery darts and then pour water over them to stop the fire.

In our Christian life the devil is attacking us. He fires doubts and temptations at us. We need to trust in God. Faith helps us to do this. What is faith? The Bible tells us: '*Now faith is the assurance of things hoped for, the conviction of things not seen*' (Hebrews 11:1).

When you trust and believe in the Lord and his Word, you have faith – a confidence that God is real. He is a spirit so you can't see him with your physical eyes, but God can give you a confidence that he is real, truthful, faithful, powerful, just and good. You will believe that God sent his Son, Jesus Christ, to take the punishment for your sin. You will believe that nothing can separate you from his love. You will have faith that you are on the winning side. Do you want faith? Ask God for it. This shield of faith will squash those pesky doubts and kick out tiresome temptations!

Helmet of Salvation

'... and take the helmet of salvation' (Ephesians 6:17).

I'm not sure which is the most important part of your body – your heart or your head. They are both pretty vital. If either your heart or head is seriously hurt, you are in danger of losing your life. That's why soldiers must wear a helmet. Cyclists need to wear helmets too. The helmet protects the brain inside your head.

I've actually got a silly slogan on my kitchen wall which says, 'Don't lose your head to gain a minute. You need your head, your brains are in it!' So let's just say your head is essential and the helmet is a very important piece of armour for a soldier.

What is the most important thing for a Christian? It is what Jesus did on the cross. Jesus died to save us from sin. This is salvation. Jesus died in the place of sinners so that those who trust in him are freed from sin's guilt and punishment for ever. Believers can trust that one day they will be without sin and will enjoy eternal life. Salvation is important. Without salvation there would be everlasting punishment. You need to experience salvation. So put on the helmet of salvation – trust in Jesus.

Sword of the Spirit

'Take the helmet of salvation, and the sword of the Spirit, which is the word of God' (Ephesians 6:17).

Not all armour is about defence. There is one important piece of armour that is about attack – the sword. Just as the belt was used to describe God's Word, so is the sword. When you read God's Word, it defends you against false beliefs and it also helps you to attack false beliefs.

You see, sometimes we will be in situations where people criticize God and his Word. We need to study God's Word so that we can stand up against those lies. We need to tell the enemies of God what God's Word says, so that they can hear it and believe and be saved.

Wonderful Women: One of the first people to see Jesus alive after his death was Mary Magdalene. In Bible times, you would never choose a woman as your chief witness. But all the first eye witnesses of Jesus' resurrection were women – this is a strong piece of evidence to show that the story of Jesus' resurrection is true and that the disciples did not make it up.

 **Think about Jesus:** We've been reading quite a bit from Ephesians chapter 6, but let's just skip back a bit to the previous chapter,

chapter 5. The first verse there says that we are to be 'imitators of God as beloved children. And walk in love as Christ loved us and gave himself up for us'. When you have a makeover, quite often you just let someone else do the job – makeup, hair etc. But God wants to change you and to have you change yourself to be like him and to be like Jesus. He particularly says in this verse that you are to love in the same way that Christ loved. Christ is the perfection of love. When we love, we usually love people who love us. But Jesus loved us while we were still sinners and didn't love him.

 **Read More:** Ephesians 6:10-20; Romans 5: 6-11

Makeover Tip: You've probably read the story of Cinderella – what a makeover story! Rags to riches. Well, the testimony of a Christian is much better. The Bible tells us that sinners are slaves to sin, but once they trust in Christ and are saved, they become heirs with Christ. Remember how earlier on we talked about how believers in Christ are part of God's family. What a turnaround! Here we have members of a royal family who used to be enemies of the head of that family. But God the Father has shown such love. He has taken these rebels and made them his own children. And he just keeps blessing and blessing and blessing. Those who trust in the Lord and Saviour Jesus Christ can look forward to a life of blessings that will last forever.

StaRting a TReNDV cRaze

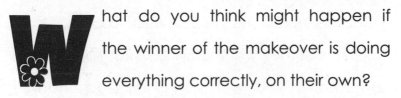hat do you think might happen if the winner of the makeover is doing everything correctly, on their own?

a. Perhaps they'll have a party?

b. Maybe the people at the party will say, 'Oh how can I get a makeover?'

c. Perhaps the makeover winner will then become the 'teacher'?

d. And a makeover craze will start across the whole neighbourhood. (It's entirely possible!)

This is one way that God works – he uses the lives of others to spread the message of his Word.

If you've come to trust in God, then your life is about worshipping God and glorifying him. One of the ways of glorifying God is by telling others about him.

God has begun a work in you that one day will be completed in heaven. You will be without sin. But as you continue to live in this world day by day, God is changing you, little by little.

People in your life will see that. You might not realise it but they will. They will watch your actions and listen to your words. And as God changes you, they will see these changes.

Some people see the changes and react negatively. They might not like it for one reason or another. Unbelievers do not have God's Holy Spirit inside them and when they see God's

Holy Spirit at work in someone else they can detest that person because they detest God.

But others react in a different way. They might ask questions because God is beginning to work in their lives too.

Just as the people at the makeover party start asking about how they can get a makeover, people who see God at work in your life might start to ask you, 'What's changed? You're different to how you were before. Perhaps you can help me? I want to have the same peace and joy you have these days.'

That would be a good time to read the Bible with them and pray. Tell them about who Jesus is and what he has done for you.

A Good Story

Now, I love a really good story ... so here's one I think you might enjoy.

There was once a scruffy old tramp who lived in a dirty little town in a dirty little shack. He slept on a rickety old bed and had nothing to wear but rags. One day something sad happened. A little girl was orphaned and he was the only one in the family who could look after her. The baby girl arrived at his home and that was when things started to change. He thought to himself, 'Now there's a little kid in the house I need to make sure the place is clean and tidy.'

He put the baby to bed and wondered where he should start. The windows seemed to be a good place to begin as they were definitely dirty. But once he had washed the glass inside the sunlight came in and he saw how really dirty the house was. He cleaned the floors and the work surfaces. He swept all the corners and tidied his bedroom. As soon as he had finished one task he found another that needed doing. Finally he got round to washing his bed sheets and when he went outside to dry them he thought, 'This garden needs weeding.' So he got a spade and dug up the thorns and thistles. He remembered he had some cans of paint in the cupboard so he began painting the fence. When that was finished he looked at himself and thought, 'Now that I've finished all this work I should spruce myself up a bit.'

That afternoon, some neighbours came for a visit and thought, 'Maybe we should tidy up a bit. It would be nice to have a garden like his.'

Be Ready

If you're a Christian that story should remind you of your life. When God showed you your sin, he started to change some things, and then others. You began to see things in your life that needed to be changed. Then other people saw these changes and thought, 'Hmm. She says that God loves her and that's what makes the difference. Perhaps I need to find out about Jesus for myself?'

When that happens be ready. The Bible tells us that we should always be ready to tell others why we trust God. What is different about you?

Remember we talked about how the Christian life is like a battle against sin?

Sometimes we don't always put up the best fight against sin. We give in too easily. But imagine you are a soldier in the olden days. You're fighting on one side, but the enemy appears to be winning. Just then a huge banner flies up in the air. Your captain has a message for you. It is emblazoned across the banner and when the army sees it they cheer. They take courage and they fight on to win the victory.

What kind of message would encourage an army to keep going? It might be 'More soldiers are coming' or 'The King has not been injured.'

What message would encourage a Christian to keep fighting against sin? The Bible is full of special messages to encourage God's people. Here's one of them: *There is therefore now no condemnation for those who are in Christ Jesus* (Romans 8:1). This message encourages Christians to continue to fight against sin because Jesus has already saved them. Jesus has already transformed them. He has performed an amazing miracle in changing them from being a sinner to being saved. And he is continuing to work in them day by day. And God is not going to punish them for their sin as Jesus has taken that punishment already.

So sit back, relax and open God's Word. Enjoy this Bible makeover. It might be hard at times. God wants you to work at it. But trust in his transforming power! When he's at work in your life you can trust that he is doing a good job.

Read More: Philippians 1:6; Romans 8; Psalm 60:4; Psalm 20:5

Wonderful Women: Now if you have trusted in Jesus Christ I want to go back to you again. ... You are wonderful. You have been made by God, saved by God and are being transformed by God. The Bible tells us that believers are the temple of the Holy Spirit. *'Do you not know that your body is a temple of the Holy Spirit within you, whom you have from God? You are not your own, for you were bought with a price. So glorify God in your body'* (1 Corinthians 6:19-20).

This transformation we've been talking about, where God saves you and equips you to be more like Christ, is an inward change that has outward consequences. The Bible tells us that we will know who the real Christians are by their lives. Read Matthew 7:16. Things will develop in your life that are proof that God is at work in you. But, although God is in charge of the makeover, you are not just a backseat passenger. You're involved. Your body is the temple of the Holy Spirit. Treat your body with respect by avoiding sin. The Bible tells us that certain sins require us to actually flee – that's a word you would use when escaping from fire, or a knife wielding maniac! Well, sin is just as serious. Even as a Christian we need to be kept from sin, delivered from temptation. God will help us, but we need to flee.

 **Think about Jesus:** When you flee from something, it's also good to flee to something. From danger to safety. So when you flee from sin and temptation

– flee to God, to Christ, to his Word! There you will find strength and rescue! Look back at 1 Corinthians 6:20 again – you were bought with a price. What a price Jesus paid to save us! Turn your love, your life, your heart, your everything over to God. Thank him for the gift of his Son, Jesus. Thank Jesus for his sacrifice. The gift of his life for you. Let God work in you!

Who is the author?

Let me introduce myself. My name is Catherine Mackenzie and I live in Inverness, in the Highlands of Scotland.

From a very early age I have loved books and stories. One day as a child the only way my parents could persuade me to take my medicine was to promise me a book. So I took a deep breath and swallowed.

Even as a child I knew that I wasn't really a Christian. I knew I didn't love Jesus in the same way as the woman who washed Jesus' feet with her tears. But several years after I read that story, I realised that I needed God's forgiveness through Jesus Christ, his Son.

These days the kid who loved to read now loves to write. The idea for this book, *How to Have a Bible Makeover* came because some girls at a summer camp I was at agreed to give me and the other leaders a pamper session. Two girls jumped at the chance of redoing my hair, face and nails. They enjoyed themselves and at the end I looked quite different! It made me think of how God wants to change me from my sinful self to someone who glorifies him and enjoys him forever.

I hope this book will help you to find out more about this wonderful, life changing God!

MY BIBLE MAKEOVER

Write down Bible verses here that will help you to become more like Jesus.

How to be a
BiBLe
PRiNCeSS

Catherine Mackenzie

How to be a Bible Princess
by Catherine Mackenzie

If you were a princess you'd have the best wardrobe in the world with new dresses in it every day – and a tiara to match. But is that all there is to being a princess? And what does it mean to be a real Bible princess? Abigail, Jehosheba, Esther and The Queen of the South were women and royalty who honoured God. Pharaoh's daughter and Michal were princesses who showed bravery, but were they true followers of the Lord? Jezebel and Herodias' daughter are two royal women who did not love God. All their stories are in the Bible and all can teach us in their own way how to be a Bible princess, daughters of the King, women and girls of righteousness.

ISBN: 978-1-84550-825-8

How to Be a Bible Beauty

Catherine Mackenzie

How to be a Bible Beauty
by Catherine Mackenzie

Some people want to look beautiful, wearing the best clothes, with gorgeous hair, and pretty jewellery. But is that what beauty is all about? Anna was devoted to God and longed to meet the promised Messiah. Leah realised that skin beauty was not as important as trusting in God for your salvation and Dorcas showed her true beauty by showing God's love to others. All these stories and others like them are in the Bible. These Bible beauties can teach us how to be women of God, people with an eternal beauty that is more than skin deep!

ISBN: 978-1-78191-578-3

God's Word and Your Life
by Laura Martin

You've got a mind – use it! If you've got questions – ask them! But don't fill your mind with rubbish and it is important to ask the right questions. The THINK, ASK – BIBLE! series uses the lives and experiences of characters from the Bible to teach important lessons. Each chapter provides opportunities to stop and think, delve into the Scriptures and be prompted with study questions. *God's Word and Your Life* covers questions about social media, money, authority, gaming, knowing God's will, and education.

ISBN: 978-1-78191-822-7

God's Word and You
by Laura Martin

You've got a mind – use it! If you've got questions – ask them! But don't fill your mind with rubbish and it is important to ask the right questions. The THINK, ASK – BIBLE! series uses the lives and experiences of characters from the Bible to teach important lessons. Each chapter provides opportunities to stop and think, delve into the Scriptures and be prompted with study questions. *God's Word and You* covers questions about friendship, work, worry, trials, family, grief, attitudes, and our bodies.

ISBN: 978-1-78191-821-0

CHRISTIAN FOCUS PUBLICATIONS

Christian Focus | Christian Heritage | CF4K | Mentor

Christian Focus Publications publishes books for adults and children under its four main imprints: Christian Focus, CF4K, Mentor and Christian Heritage. Our books reflect our conviction that God's Word is reliable and Jesus is the way to know him, and live for ever with him.

Our children's publication list includes a Sunday School curriculum that covers pre-school to early teens, and puzzle and activity books. We also publish personal and family devotional titles, biographies and inspirational stories that children will love.

If you are looking for quality Bible teaching for children then we have an excellent range of Bible stories and age-specific theological books.

From pre-school board books to teenage apologetics, we have it covered!

Find us at our web page:
www.christianfocus.com

CF4•K
Because you're never too young to know Jesus